Leaves of a Diary

by Flavia Cosma

Translation by Matt Loftin with the author

Leaves of a Diary 7, 25, 26, 32, 46 first appeared in Absinthe –
New European Writing, #4, June 2005.
Leaves of a Diary
All original work © 2006 by Flavia Cosma
All rights reserved under International and Pan-American Copyright Convention.
The use of any part of this publication reproduced, transmitted in any form or by any means, electronic, mechanical, photocopying, recording or otherwise stored in a retrieved system, without the prior consent of the publisher is an infringement of the copyright law.

Library and Archives Canada Cataloguing in Publication

Cosma, Flavia
Leaves of a diary / Flavia Cosma ; translator, Matt Loftin and Flavia Cosma.

Translated from the Romanian.
Poems.

I. Loftin, Matt II. Title.

PS8555.O676L42 2006   *C859'.1*   *C2006-901195-8*

ISBN 0-9689561-7-3

Publisher: Dae-Tong Huh
Design & Layout: Sandra Huh
Cover Design: Sandra Huh

Korean-Canadian Literary Forum-21 Press
PO BOX 45035
5845 Yonge St.
Willowdale, ON M2M 4K3 Canada
Phone: 416.222.7935
email: varietycrossing@gmail.com

Printed and bound in Canada

FLAVIA COSMA
www.flaviacosma.com

SELECTED PUBLICATIONS

ENGLISH

FATA MORGANA, poems, 2003 Edwin Mellen Press, Lewiston, NY, ISBN 0-7734-3482-8, 87 pages.
WORMWOOD WINE, poems, 2004, 2001, Edwin Mellen Press, Lewiston, NY, ISBN 0-7734-3416-X, ISBN 0-7734-3553-0 (hc), 87 pages.
THE FIRE THAT BURNS US, a novel, 1996, Singular Speech Press, Canton, Connecticut, ISBN 1-880286-34-3, 114 pages.
47 POEMS, 1992, Texas Tech University Press, ISBN 089672-304-6, ISBN 0-89672-279-1, 99 pages.
FAIRY TALES by Flavia Cosma, 1990, Canadian Stage and Arts, Toronto, Canada, ISBN 0-919952-48-8, 47 pages.

ROMANIAN

RHODES, RHODOS ORI RODI, Jurnal Sentimental, (Travel Memoir), Oct. 2005, Editura Limes, Cluj, Romania, ISBN 973-726-093-7, 150 pages
JURNAL, poems, 2004, Cogito Press, Oradea, Romania, ISBN 973-8032-35-0, 68 pages
AMAR DE PRIMAVARA (BITTERNESS OF SPRING), poems, 2003, Romania Libera Press, Bucharest, Romania, ISBN 973-86308-8-6, 83 pages
CINA CU DEMONI (DINING WITH DEMONS), poems, 1999, Eminescu Press, Bucharest, Romania, ISBN 973-22-0759-0, 91 pages
PASARI SI ALTE VISE (BIRDS AND OTHER DREAMS), poems, 1997, Eminescu Press, Bucharest, Romania, ISBN 973-22-0589-X, 84 pages

AWARDS:

1. ALTA Richard Wilbur Prize for Poetry in Translation for" 47 POEMS", 1989 (Translations by Dr. Don Wilson with the author)
2. Canadian Scene National Award for the TV Documentary "ROMANIA A COUNTRY AT THE CROSSROADS", 1991
3. PRIMER PREMIO – PAZ EN EL MUNDO – PRIMER CONCURSO POEMAS POR LA PAZ – ARGENTINA, Bilingual Writers MCA, for the poem The Season of Love (Spanish and English versions) February 2005

Acknowledgments

This book was finalized in the beautiful island of Rhodes, courtesy of The International Writers' and Translators' Centre of Rhodes. Grateful thanks.

*To all who generously squander
Moment to moment
The Eternity.*

Flavia Cosma's "Leaves of a Diary"
(`a la maniere de Lisa Robertson*)
11/11/MMIV

        In Ottawa this morning, in a West-glancing room
Of this Gothic hotel, the Chateau Laurier,
Surveying the canal locks and their mercurial water,
Saturated with the "cold damp day" the weather woman
Announces for us citizens, remembering—
(Under the fallout of drizzle and dizzy leaves,
Not far from the Parliament edifices, un-edifying)
Our old people's sacrifices in the *film noir* wars,
Whose survivors prick their own hearts with poppies,
Stabbing black, grey, or dark-blue coats with a scarlet wound,
As brilliant as the national flag, but dearer,
There can only be surrender to what owns us—
This dreary meteorology, plus the tyrannous, star-crossed astrology:
Is there any remedy in poetry, Flavia?
        Romanian-Canadian singer, I peel and leaf
Your *Leaves of a Diary*, these tantalizing, entrancing
Translations into English of a Latin language, one
I hear from you, when you speak or recite, is so beautiful,
These *belle-lettres* against our bellicose trilling
Of war, war, war. Maybe that's why these verses sound
So achingly of Anna Akhmatova (née Gorenko),
Who heard and recited the creepy tragedy of Gulag elegies—
Even as I hear the Poe-like chimes of the Peace Tower
Hitting at 11h, *onze heure*, 11A.M., 11 O'Clock,
On all four faces of the clock tower, scaring us
Into revery of bleeding and screams, of sobs
Mangling multilingual grief. Maybe that's why
I also see in your imagist 'fairy' tales glimpses
Of that shy, mysterious, US Civil War poet
Who refuses to talk about the carnage, namely,
Emily Dickinson of the primal metaphysics,
The impassioned airs, the impish arias…
(One requires soldiers' eyes to detect Dickinson's
Raw-meat soul and carnal spirituals).

~//~

Now the national television broadcasts
"The Last Post" sounded on a silver-colored,
Silver-toned, silver-tongued trumpet, and I see
The Governor-General and Consort saluting
The Tomb of the Unknown Soldier, overflowing
With citizens' respectfully discarded poppies,
And now four cannon—olive-drab under grey rain—
Take turns shattering the air above
The House of Commons and the Senate,
Shooting orange flames that blossom into blue smoke,
While concussions, percussive, shake me
Three seconds before the same shots echo
From this TV set. The delay doubles the shock:
That's economy. Righteously scared birds explode upwards
Into the gray gloom outside, like shrapnel,
And now a bagpipe chorus answers the thudding gunning,
With needles of notes: a vain opera.
      But Flavia, it's not just Akhmatova and Dickinson
Your glamorous lyricism trumpets, but also that Québécois poetess,
Marie Uguay, now sadly as dead as Plath, though
I believe it was from cancer, not suicide,
Way back in fatal 1981, and not before
She had finished wry, solemn, surrealistic epigrams,
That detonated into Canuck English as unignorably
As those assassins' bullets entered Ceauşescu.
      Listen! Here's Mary Ann Burdett
Of the Royal Canadian Legion reciting lines
Wrested from John McCrae's "In Flanders Fields,"
(Anglo-Canada's most famous poem, a deathly one, naturally).
      Ah, Flavia, your poetry recovers the Gospel of Paul,
A possibility for salvation, for resurrection, right out of
Collisions of contradiction. Ain't there such soft
Questioning, harsh love, fragrant evil, plush divinity,
Curious hurt, maimed innocence, angry flavors,
Political plagues, anorexia nervosa, manic
Depression, morbid boredom, sooty morals,
Champagne blues, gilded muck, delirium tremens,

Melancholy alcohol, dazzling terror, storybook spasms,
Drowsy murderers, tar-stuck stars, classic bleeding,
Sweaty bliss, vinegar'd sunlight, cyanide nectar, *et cetera*,

$$\sim//\sim$$

In your snapshots of vulturous angels, clumsy vampires,
Leprous lyres, obscene perfumes, and nests of pain?
        To read you is to excavate *Beauty*
Despite the dictates of butchery,
The theology of our trenches,
While outside the mourning throngs disperse
To the freedom of credit cards and shopping malls
And the Royal Bank *über alle*,
And sunlight dribbles down between the rain
Repeated,
Repeated.

George Elliott Clarke
Department of English
University of Toronto

Contents

Leaves of a Diary 1..........................17
Leaves of a Diary 2..........................18
Leaves of a Diary 3..........................19
Leaves of a Diary 4..........................20
Leaves of a Diary 5..........................21
Leaves of a Diary 6..........................22
Leaves of a Diary 7..........................23
Leaves of a Diary 8..........................24
Leaves of a Diary 9..........................25
Leaves of a Diary 10........................26
Leaves of a Diary 11........................27
Leaves of a Diary 12........................28
Leaves of a Diary 13........................29
Leaves of a Diary 14........................30
Leaves of a Diary 15........................31
Leaves of a Diary 16........................32
Leaves of a Diary 17........................33
Leaves of a Diary 18........................34
Leaves of a Diary 19........................35
Leaves of a Diary 20........................36
Leaves of a Diary 21........................38
Leaves of a Diary 22........................40
Leaves of a Diary 23........................41
Leaves of a Diary 24........................42
Leaves of a Diary 25........................43

Contents

Leaves of a Diary 26..........................44
Leaves of a Diary 27..........................45
Leaves of a Diary 28..........................46
Leaves of a Diary 29..........................47
Leaves of a Diary 30..........................48
Leaves of a Diary 31..........................49
Leaves of a Diary 32..........................50
Leaves of a Diary 33..........................51
Leaves of a Diary 34..........................52
Leaves of a Diary 35..........................53
Leaves of a Diary 36..........................54
Leaves of a Diary 37..........................55
Leaves of a Diary 38..........................56
Leaves of a Diary 39..........................57
Leaves of a Diary 40..........................58
Leaves of a Diary 41..........................59
Leaves of a Diary 42..........................60
Leaves of a Diary 43..........................61
Leaves of a Diary 44..........................62
Leaves of a Diary 45..........................63
Leaves of a Diary 46..........................64
Leaves of a Diary 47..........................65
Leaves of a Diary 48..........................66
Leaves of a Diary 49..........................67
Leaves of a Diary 50..........................68
Leaves of a Diary 51..........................69
And Now the World........................70

1

The pain intoxicates you like wine,
You flow into immeasurable caves,
Where naked bodies wildly coil
And Satan's pitchfork
Skewers your chest.

Who is the stranger with the stony forehead?
What fresh depressions haunt
His lost-angel face
And his smile, - a mask-?
What passed through him
While I was sleeping
With my breath heavy,
Prolonged?

2

The warm wind of the golden autumn
Whirls the curtains with pallid light,
And for a split second envelops the room
Like a wing of an angel
In flight.

Lying still, I drink the tardy sap
At once, with my whole being,
As I did in my grandparents' coarse bed
When the sugared aroma of unyeasted hay
Would fortify me.

3

We sit on the stony edge of the world,
Half asleep,
              half aware,
Sensing, Seeing,
Flood waves,
Gaping earth,
Mortars,
The End
Nearing us.

Jesus, pierced
              on His cross,
Presses longing lips to us
And waits.

4

I excavated the entire summer
On the tepid fields,
Around mice and ashen snakes.
I dug, burying every wish
In a blind well
Run dry.

5

The sun comes to me occasionally
With soft fingers on the windowpane.
Its rays, - shafted bundles-,
Rush through my veins
With the same grounded joy.

Among flowers and seeds,
I smile to myself
Out of the square, dreamy frames.

6

When embarrassed, I catch
                     my sobs in my throat
And ask myself what
Has been so pitiful; the razing nights
That have passed are but simple strayings.

In the water-bellied sky
The silhouette of a smoky love
-Tired rainbow-
Hangs about
Thinly.

Confused, I stare into mirrors
At the dark ridges on my quiet face,
At the heavy bite, the deep seals,
Whirlings of some today
That I hardly remember.

7

The sun, tepid salver,
Burned molasses flames into Autumn's lap,
The sky unraveled
In incandescent strips;
The signs began to show themselves at sunset—
It rained red apples on the fields.

Serenity, gorgeous, eternal,
Poured its tender milk over the valleys;
From the houses scattered on the hillocks,
Light rippled in ember eyes.

Sinewy branches, painted with shadows,
Held fastened, arched in the twilight;
A heron soared
Over waters.

My dreams, wild pigeons,
Slept helplessly on wiry beds of fairy tales;
Fleshy, bluish plums
Oozed, burdened by the rains;
Naught and never-
Everlasting, hexed words,
Kept a solemn vigil
Over the silence between us.

8

The moon,
Which I had not seen for some time,
Glides on the vault, a proud maiden.
Instead of shinning over paved cities,
Thickets turned wild
And large lakes,
She stands straight above the sea and on seashores,
Always young, still the same frowning queen.
Only her golden hair appears more coppery,
And her tears falling into muddy waters,
Are scarlet, like the sacred fire's embers
That flicker throughout times
                      and unspent,
Keep watch over ancient dwelling places
Widowed now of bustle and of tribes.

9

In the fall
You're dearer to me than ever.
The season softly collects you,
In dozen of anonymous faces,
Exhausted from exertion.

Your hair, fresh hay from the plain,
Shines warm rays of the past summer,
Your eyes, ailing suns,
Burn through lowly fogs
With incensed fevers.

A lithe prince,
A wandered dream,
You scatter with the hoarfrost in the morning.
The youthful cold radiantly shapes you
Into fragile sheets of ice.

Spent, syruped time passes by,
The sob yeasts in our chests like a dough.
I fall into a well of memories,
Thrashing the withered air
With my hands, hopeless wings.

10

Red eyelids hide a fiery eye
Under distant smoky clouds.
A perfect line rims the horizon,
The sky fills up with small surf.

Huge willows bend with rusted leaves,
Heavy armors, golden, weeping,
Majestic curtains
Opening
A secret path
That, in the world of yellow wonders
Humbly, I steal upon.

11

The tamed mountains
Ribbon roads. We glide through them
Dreamlike. The bluish humps
Stripped of leaves envelop us
With round shadows,
Nesting us.

The blue-gray light
Tempers flames within our quiet selves.
Shy descends over our eyelids,
And kisses our shameful sorrows,
A sweet sister
Soothing our hidden wounds
With night's fingers.

We are urged to forget
The dared soaring,
The strong air trickling in our lungs,
The exhaustion made of gold,
The heroic act,
The neverending sky,
The future.

Descending farther
On the blue and gray ridges,
We immerse ourselves in the blind embrace,
Both warm and colorless alike,
Without crying,
Without thinking.

12

Under a bridge with ten wings
Leaf fires smolder
In nests made of stone.

The valley breathes mists
On a belated passion.

The sadness of events
Yet to come
Is tempting me sweetly.

13

How transparent the sun
In a grape's skin!

How full the apples,
Wild and sleeping
Under the aged tree!

How dark the seeds
On the sidewalk,
Willed by the wind!

Even pale, purple pansies
Know the icy kiss
     of the moon,
The thrilled breath in darkness,
The rain in fine drops, like memories,
The worries, the horseflies.
Invisible hands graced them
Gathering
Some dahlias, some mimosas.

We talk about the dead at midnight
As if they are alive and with us,
We tenderly talk with the living
As if they are dead,
     still loved.
The caressing flames
Flicker amid our words
Now in one world,
Now in the other.

14

Don't wholly open your eyes
And keep the windows drawn half-closed.
Do not believe, Oh, do not believe;
Many people rush the light,
Demolish the gates diligently,
Invade the suns with their addled thoughts,
Seizing afterward
The stars and moon
One after another.

In the holy room, they merrily party,
Even in the gardens of the heavens they feast,
Leaving in their wake shards of glass, bones
                                    and bracelets,
Empty promises, trash of the earth.

It is wiser to keep your eyes shut,
To prevent that dirty rain from soaking you.
Don't let the sand, dust rummaged by the wind,
Splash your blossoms, your wreath,
So your large eyes – dropping star-girls
May be spared the tears
Of blood and clay.

15

The storm is nearing
 In white beginnings.
The wind twirls
Hungry under windows,
As the poplar struggles,
Risen by its armpits,
Gnashing with frozen branches
To undo its own dream
And smash its nests.

And the bird gets drunk
In the building whirlwind,
Lets its small body carry
Into the hurricane,
Swallowing with relish
At the boundless strength.
In the endless second,
It passes, lightly,
From the great crush
To hoarfrost eternity.

16

During insomniac nights
We discover tombs
Of dreamy emperors and kings,
Treasures secreted in caves,
Fatigued skeletons,
Lives passed in loving concealment
Over which the whitened dust
Settles its protective sheen.

And who are we?
When did we become bold,
Spiritless to disturb
            their endless sleep,
With thirst to reveal
Unspoken secrets
And the blind hope
To somehow understand.

17

I am given silks and laces,
Foamy garments, refreshing,
Their aroma adorn my house
With majestic folds and waves.

I also receive fur-lined mantles,
Tediously stitched from rare animal hides,
That lightly envelop my ankle;
With vaporous shadows
They kiss my face
And set on my head decadent tiaras
Of precious stones and gold,
Their light, ruby, blue,
Pierces the day's white
With charmed rays.

But God, what do I do
With these lush temptations?
Snares whose time has left me;
My courtyards are bereft of uproars,
My rooms emptied
Of galas and rulers.
On the hollow road
With my dreams humbled,
I return to You
    as at the on-set,
So that from these earthly passions
With great wisdom,
And kind heart, You will deliver me.

18

A large bird
Made a stop at the window,
On a branch black from frost.
It was so big,
        so blue,
That we fancied it
A messenger from above.

But why was it standing
With its back to us,
        thoughtful
On the leafless branch?
We had expected it to perform a miracle,
Speak to us in parables,
Or more clearly, to fly away.

The omen, if omen it was,
Halfway untold
Sows unease
In our brittled minds;
Prayers started and forgotten
Return to us midday
As new sins
That wander our lives
        and unknown courses,
—Birds waiting patient on the branch—
As wild expectations,
As blue beginnings.

19

In the dark
        all things seem newer,
                more beautiful.
Bodies loosen—lankier, lightened,
Smiles gather heat and mirth,
Hands again find the shadowed edge of dreams.

In the dark the grass is sprouting
From withered, ashen seeds.
Transparent blankets drape the horizon
With mysterious, blue snow.

20

At the edge of the thought
Has piled garbage:
Remainders of prolonged feasts,
Withered, fetid, heaps,
Dreams of night, the blind testimonies.

Holly and dear Mother,
Pure as a beam,
Forgive me again,
That I brazenly dared
To come to You and pray to You on my knees
Without beforehand
Having swept and gathered
That dissipated summer waste
And humbly washed my eyes
Of jaded tears.

With unflinching will,
I obstinately banged
At closed gateways
So You would deliver me
And give me what I couldn't forever have,
My path differently harvested.

Needy the soul now turns
Face to the wall and waits
For actualization of the hour
              that anyhow was due,
And You return
Merciful to Your tasks
And forget about me, not even understanding
That my heart clinches, a red fist,
And the foreordained stone
Weights on me more
Every time I see myself –
Who I now am—
In the light of Your blue
And limpid
Quiet ray.

21

Many times I asked myself
About the endless sleep;
Sometimes with fear, sometimes without patience.
How will the thread of life
Be set with these expensive jewels:
Truth standing
On its renowned place,
Justice, modest ornament,
Amid other things, and
                equally precious,
The endless beginning.

And I asked myself again
About the arms of the Father
Lightly descending with us in the depth,
About the fine rain
Stealing across the face
Through gray layers of earth;
Will the clouds cry? Will they talk?
Maybe it will even snow in the height of the summer.
Sadness sifted
From the sonorous sorrows
Envelops the blue flowers
With silky shrouds.

People still visit
The same grave,
Seldom, more seldom, no haste,
Steps echo in the alleyways.
The cemetery lies in wait with eyes of oblivion
For a butterfly,
A tender word.
The Holly Book remains open
At the page of those without Spirit.
The bones sleep, white
Under the sandy soil.
The light rummages through the midday.
The souls are detached of passion.
The sleep is big,
Beautiful.

22

Like a burst of pitch
Spouting into clouds,
Black birds tear away from branches;
Pouncing, tumbling over us,
Petals in mourning, ill omens.

Frozen, late grass
Is ground by hungry beaks,
Clowns beckon to us,
                obscenely,
Enticing us
With gloved hands.

Sister Death, at the window, predicts evil;
In the vast ether
Your voice lingers.

23

The snow-less winter
Breathes, long-winded,
Like an endless autumn
With no sun.
On the gray sky,
An eye of rainbow
—Round coin—
Intermittently appears.

During the nameless winter,
We dream of immense snow banks,
Of tender hands on the head's crown,
Of warm lights, flickering.
We dream that together, we fall asleep
Sheltered, far away.

24

I hear footsteps yet again,
Heavy footsteps, pressed to the ground.

Somebody is walking through the house.

I hear artful steps,
The whispering steps of a cat.

Somebody is coming up the stairs.

I hear the shuffling steps
Of a monk at Lent.
I get very frightened
By shining, black-shoed steps,
By funereal steps.

Toward the morning
Time straightens its back.
Its steps are trampling us
All-embracing.

We're setting the table
With bread made of stone.
Heavy weeping descends
From the clouds filled sky.

The steps keep time
In the chilly room.
Stale, food thickens on the plate.
Day, shuttered in,
Slowly spends itself.
Why?
What I am waiting for?
And who
Is there still to come?

25

The city's lights trouble me
Like a dirty,
            brazen thought
Lanterns, lit in the doorways,
Mark the grand turn
Of centuries,
From the second millennium
To the second void.

The city's lights follow me,
Yellow, magnificent fans,
In bunches—cheerful beams
                that tempt me
With twinkling,
Cunning eyelashes.

26

My heart sometimes explodes
A noisily smashed urn
                from which
Thousands of drops, colored garlands, gush.
Arcs unfurl, glide into emptiness,
A starry array of hearts,
Faultless, shinning.

The void fills itself, disappears
Under my infinite heart
Which in flight stabs the absence
With golden, stellar rays.

27

On the way to the city,
I race, scrambling with the shadows,
On the winding and stony road;
Hurriedly, I wrestle with the shadows
Who leap in my path to swiftly encircle me;
Cut my breath
              until
In my turn,
I descend into a shadow.

I float aimlessly, idle ghost,
Like the dance of deep waters at nightfall.
Phantoms, embittered and famished,
Skirmish, kill each other,
While, shining on the horizon,
The city of dreams bathes in light.

28

The road stays, sated, white,
Stretched out, facing the sky.
Rare snowflakes slowly descend,
The branch keeps mum,
A nest laid bare.

The river lifts its shirt at the shores,
Runs higher and higher on its fleet feet,
Runs hurriedly with the fish and the shadows.

Trice slips the footstep
On snow-hidden ice;
Mirrors slyly gleam beneath the flimsy cover;
The horizon teems with eyes and snares;
We christen each other with high reverence,
We want the recollection of who it is we are
To carry us forward.

29

A dead hand hovers, perched above me,
Wants to ruffle the strands
              on my forehead, as though in jest.
It playfully disturbs the air, cold fingers
Adorned with precious and heavy rings.

The lifeless hand boldly
Obstinates above my head,
              floats,
In passing touches me with a slight flutter,
Reminds me of worlds submerged long ago,
Of parallel lives.

30

I fall into sleep as in another world,
Subterranean or extraterrestrial,
A world with foreign laws and customs,
With mysterious temples and hills.

Strange things are happening there
But they don't astonish us in the least.
On the streets we meet with unknown throngs,
Who we feel we have seen before
In our day-to-day life.

And if out of the blue
The miracle should happen,
O, if we'd regain
The keys to the tall gates,
We'd keep them open between sleep and watchfulness,
We would understand everything, all at once,
The past,
And the future,
Wandering time and the vastness;
Leisurely and wise
We'd sate ourselves
On a tree of bitter, ripened fruit.

31

Snowflakes pounced at the car windows,
Smashed against frozen pane
To crumble on the road and then to stand again.
Gathering their cursing in hurried counsel,
With its breast white and withered by high winds
The highway, unleashed, raced
Towards a certain place unseen in the distance,
Like the frog who preordained dashes
Toward the open mouth of a snake, and jumps.

32

I hear soft taps
Whispered in my ear;
May be my rib cage
Tossing on the pillow,
Breathing, exhaling?

Could it be just my heart
A slack medusa, pulsating,
Into a sea tinted red,
Like the sun
At dusk?

Or maybe there are rivers,
Large ones, hidden ones,
Blue lines, flowing
On ring shaped geographies.

Yet, I still believe, Lord,
That they are your little angels,
Merrily jumping around
When the silence, like a cat,
Purrs by the stove's side,
And the moon, a pale forehead,
Emerges from waves, at night.

Mindful, the steps enter
Stealthily, into the room,
Searching for places fit for a slumber;
Weary are the angels after the storm!

Calm overcomes us all
With bony, blessed hands,
Hands of a loving grandmother.

33

The wind races madly over the hills
Like time that grouts scraggy brows,
The snowflakes circle in tender dance,
The frost descends at midnight;
Winter's blanket spreads over the houses
Wistfully.

Unknown pains pierce the monotony
With severe, invisible daggers:
Is this, perhaps, the hour?
Is this, perhaps, the moment?
Fright bites us hard;
The wings, heavy with question, stop flight.

34

I find myself always warm
In the laps of pine trees, ruffled, green,
Even when winter with its elongated fingers,
Descends forcefully from the clouds,
The tears of Saint Anthony
Weep unbroken on the drained faces,
And the world trembles
                    from its foundation.

Away from fear I roll and fall asleep
In nests of pine trees, sweetly scented,
Soft shadows enwrap me with much care
In the warmth of a mother,
In a warmth of a brother,
In the misty warmth
Of a lover.

35

The snowfall seizes us, traps
With a cold and humid soft cloth,
And like an unseen spider
Wraps us up in a graying shroud;
Fastened molecules in icy spheres
Under great billows, a divine jail,
That, from distances,
Seems white, pure,
A vast, shining appearance.

36

In the amorphous city,
Blackened by crimes, passions,
By perspiration dripped in waves on the pavement,
Three generations lull themselves to sleep, humming
A song about the Aegean Sea;
In their green dream,
Seated, barefoot,
 at the water's edge,
On the lip of history, they contemplate
The time that passes.

The river whispers lazily downstream,
The song trickles through dusty air;
Under cupolas of transvestite churches
The thought gets inebriated from weighty longings,
Hearts start contentedly
In the rustling of blessed willows.

37

They have told us that, toward the evening,
The moon will disappear
Among snow banks and speeding cars,
That its place will be assumed
By modest artificial lights.
Puzzled, we wander
Among the bluish, giant buildings
        that hunt harmony in the depths;
The wind freezes tears on the soft corners of eyelashes,
Frost reddens our faces;
Overwhelmed by anxiety, we lay waiting
For dark signs on the sky.

We scent in the air a beamed breath,
Fortifying, everlasting like a rustle on the plain,
A breath, omni powerful and blue,
A new spring, like the springs
Of which, tenderly,
Our grandparents reminisced.

38

How You managed to wither me, Lord with the frost!
What did You give me to drink, what wormwood wine,
So that I forgot the fiery thirst,
The hot thigh,
The smile?

How will I be able to receive
Your gifts, Lord,
Now that the warm sun,
After many winters,
Mounts the hill?

39

I have learned how to follow
The straight line in a labyrinth.
I know the correct answer
To every angle of a question.

It is as though
I observe from afar
Blind miracles.

It is as though
I no longer lack something.

In flight,
I shove myself against new laws
Floating through air, forever shifting
Like thousands of colored kites
Dropped from the arms of child-like adults.

All fall into the blue net of the sky.
Turned upside down,
The fulcrum
Gravitates continually
On a dirty, crawling axis,
With a weak wing
And a burdened mind.

40

When love moves on
A beam on traveling horizons,
From the starless vault
A pale angel disappears.

We bury him gently in a fairy tale's leaves
And look forward to find him again, a loner
In the perpetual march of mirrored worlds,
When walking barefoot through slurry snow,
We will have to tell him the truth
About the terrible, ill-fated occurrence;
How we unwillingly left him to die
And then how we, emptied archangels,
Fell out of Heaven.

41

Let me sprout
In a slim furrow under heavy snow,
Where it is still cold outside,
With warring winds,
But where I like your world,
Its fortressed walls.

Branches and sighs,
Whitened by winter,
Release themselves again
To the mercy of divine whispers.

Colors of soft cloth
Welcome me through the doorway,
One half cries, another waits.
I alone hurry to freedom
And the harsh, fleshy green
Surrounds me as clothes and love.

When loneliness with its light
Greets me on the road in the morning,
A new promise
Makes its way toward my mind,
The unbeaten path seduces me,
The mind remains locked, a bird-cage.

Birds made of colored paper
Flutter their wings on warmed branches,
The insects wake up in alien places,
The flowers raise, stand up,
Cheerfully the wind lectures us,
With its frail arms
Gathering from times past
Future solitudes.

43

Of all the forms
That lie at the world's foundation,
The one most spiritless
Is geometry,
Perfection of sleep,
An infinite path,
A motionless, straight line.

With coarse geometry
The city presses me to its stony chest.

In springtime,
Light crashes its cold walls
Like a perplexed bird,
Fragile songbird.

44

The angel took my hand
And for hours guided me along streets,
                            among graves.
I felt his fearful palm in mine
And on my face his wing, light, ardent.

I was looking for a certain place, a token of peace,
A silver-faced tombstone.
He already knew its location,
But let me walk
At random,
His shadow beside me, fragile, wise.

He finally took me to my target
And in quietness laid around me until evening,
When, with childish smile and tender joy,
He released me from my passions,
                        allowed me to the angels.

They say that there are many roads untravelled by the mind
And twisted wires that pair our cells,
Masterly weavings on the vaulted brain
That drive us on rutted paths.

What do they know about clusters of angels?
Or their blue-colored kingdom?

45

There are paths forbidden from the present,
There are hands forever untouched,
There are eyes that don't want
To look in mine anymore,
There are flowers of stone.

Time pulls me in its wake, slowly,
Without asking my opinion,
Careless of my hands
              that stretch to the world,
Of the heart fully stricken,
Of the famished skin,
              deliberately.

The velvet dream
Visits me nightly
To cradle me with soft smoke wings,
And, like smoke, trickles at dawn
Into the calm, nameless day.

46

Why all these tears
When winter has passed?
What longings weigh on you like a blanket spread
Over times, over ridges?
What hard disease at your mind's root
Drizzles your buds
With belated poison?

47

Burnt stone, burnt stone,
When will you let the rain wash your face?
When will you abandon your countless worries
And allow the warm grain
To blossom within your belly
With its fire flower?

48

The mountains, perfect and multiple breasts
Ascend to far places in the sky,
Rust-color and wiry silk
Covers them, a rustled cloak
With the sharp longings
        of woods.

49

Buds and birds
Burst voluptuously through the helpless air,
Gentle trills tickle the sky's ears,
Green tassels kiss our foreheads,
The resurrected play
              lures us again.

Blinded, we stretch our hands to the world;
The unsure passion scarcely flickers,
Pallid hands hold us tight by the coat-sleeves.
We are many, sightless;
We don't want to be lost
Into the silver obscurity.

50

Warmed cotton clouds
Embrace the crooked smile,
The soul crouched in a corner,
The mice that dance over the world,
Wild greens.

Both life and the crying,
Twin stones,
            skip on the waves,
Tears are needy, salted;
The line drawn between truth and lie
Hazes beneath moon ray,
Shadows shoulder the space between dream and nightmare,
Our paths disappear in the spring.

Oh! Old age with no boundaries!
How white the sky, the nothing!
How tired the eyes
When searching
      always searching,
           and searching.

51

These leaves will end in spring,
Melted in the boiler with dampened snows.
Stately pines will shake themselves
And, suddenly green,
Will carry on high
Their entire pride.

These thoughts close themselves, circles,
Gracefully dancing on the bluish vault,
Mysterious, phosphorescent spheres,
Dreaming stars,
Round rainbows.

Gliding across the sky
Like the moon's chicks
Now snowflakes,
Raindrops,
Then down of feathered angels.

And Now the World…

Beyond the void made of frigid marble
Where I live without bridges,
Without clothing,
An entire world waits with patience.
Lithe paths emerge under extended palms;
Astonished windows open
                        toward the sun,
Flocks of birds follow me wherever I go
In a hanging, singing,
Train.

I, like people with plentiful destinies,
Am content to replace
A longing with a new sadness,
A worry with another
                larger one.

MATT LOFTIN

Matt Loftin is a writer and teacher of writing. He graduated from Iowa State University with a M.A. in English in 2001, and was the recipient of the *Pearl Hogrefe Fellowship* from that university in 1999. He presently lives and works in Huston, TX and is daydreaming of teaching English in Buenos Aires.

Leaves of a Diary